The Transformatio
to Happii

GW01043896

Introduction	4
Neuroplasticity – Rewiring in Response to Experience	8
How Processes Saved My Life	11
Who Are You?	19
Areas of Life	25
Building Self Esteem and Confidence	28
Mindfulness and the Ego	36
Positivity	39
Gratitude	41
Friends	42
The Past	44
The Present	46
The Future	46
Anger	49
Forgiveness	51
Guilt	53
Health and Diet	55
Attachment	57
Letting Go	58
Mirror Work	59
Mindfulness Process	62
The Negative Voice	63

Shame from School   64

Bullying   66

Self-Limiting Beliefs   66

How Do You See The Image Of Yourself   69

Circle of Excellence   70

Completing the Past   70

The Power of Giving   74

Re-framing Traumatic Events   75

The Beginning   82

The 12 Karmic Laws   83

Introduction

Transformation is a very interesting phenomenon. It is a process that requires a set of procedures, exercises or techniques to take you out of your normal mindset. We seem at times to be stuck in a particular way of thinking, or in an environment that just doesn't suit us. Any effort to change how we think, feel, or behave appears futile. It is as though we lack the mental strength to break out of a dense shadow, that we have been carrying for years. This is no surprise to anyone that works with patients with behavioural problems. They often see that behaviour is directly linked to the neural networks that were wired when we were younger. In order to change a persons behaviour, they understand that they must work to transform the patterns locked into their neural pathways.

For years psychologists have been researching mental behaviour and its relation to the mind. From this research we are able to create new techniques and processes that alter mental behaviour at the neural level. Only when we can change the neural pathways, can we be free of restrictive negative patterns and behaviours.

For a few people these patterns do not restrict what they can do in life. For others however, it can stop them from succeeding, cause depression, create addictions, lead to stress, and in some cases, it can cause them to commit suicide. When negative patterns are in place, it is as if people take on a different identity, forgetting who they are and what they stand for. Many people that have had a huge emotional reaction caused by a negative pattern, report that it was as if they were a different person. For some people, negative patterns are a daily occurrence leading to anxiety, stress, and depression for most of the time.

Self-limiting beliefs are also thought to be created to a large extent in early age. Neural pathways form quickly in children, as they have nothing to compare against. This is different for adults because they can rationalise, as they have experiences to reference. Children that are criticised, put down, or laughed at, often don't already have enough positive neural pathways to negate the effect of these negative actions.

Wherever you are in terms of your negative patterns and self-limiting beliefs, there are ways to rid yourself of their burden. Transformational techniques are the most successful strategy I have ever come across for achieving happiness.

To give you an example, I will first tell you a little about who I used to be as a person and how I became that way. As far back as I can remember my childhood was devoid of any love. My parents were cold, there was no touch, no cuddles, no bedtime stories, or any minor signs of affection. As a child, this left me craving attention. It is no surprise that at the age of 7, I was sent to a psychiatrist with behavioural problems. I was cutting holes in random objects with scissors to name one. On another occasion whilst staying at my Aunties house, I put all the ornaments in the room into my bed. I have no recollection of doing this, but I can see how as a child I reacted based on the negative patterns that had been created early on.

Later in life my relationships with women were very stressful and I was anxious most of the time I wasn't with them. My lack of love and affection had created a pattern that had led me to believe that affection would be withheld, and that I was not worthy of it. As a result, I was constantly afraid that the relationship would end. I was also painfully shy and found it very difficult to talk in social circles. It took me many years and many courses to find the transformational techniques that worked for me. Now you can't keep me quiet, and my relationships are definitely much smoother.

The great thing about transformational techniques, is that they can work on a level you are mostly unaware of. Some can bring up emotions and cause strong reactions, whilst others are silent in their work and this is unseen to our conscious mind. So how do transformational processes work? To answer this, we must look at the science behind the mind and neuroplasticity.

Neuroplasticity – Rewiring in Response to Experience

"*One form of neuroplasticity is involved in learning and memory -- a fundamental form of human cognition -- but then there are lots of other forms of neuroplasticity that we're interested in how they act in health and disease.*" -- Prof Anthony Hannan

Neuroplasticity is derived from two words, neuron and plastic. A neuron refers to the nerve cells in our brain. Plastic refers to the ability to change or mould the nerve cells. Neuroplasticity refers to the process the brain goes through to change its neural pathways in order to adapt to new information, whether that is knowledge, trauma, or a change in environment. As we learn new things our brain does some organising, almost like filing, so that we are able to easily recall those pathways. A good example would be what happened in our brain when we learnt to ride a bike. The level of concentration we had to maintain in order to keep from falling off. Bit by bit after repeating the same process, our brain built neural pathways and they were strengthened each time we got back on the bike. Eventually, there were enough neural pathways created to take care of what our hands do, what our feet do, where we look, how we move, and how they all interact with the part of the brain that connects to the ears to help us stay upright. We literally grew neural pathways by performing this repeated behaviour. We now know that the brain is constantly removing and replacing the individual connections within the brain. The process known as "synaptic pruning" occurs depending on how the area of the brain is being used. This is how we are able to feed our brain new data where our negative patterns and self-limiting beliefs reside, and reprogram these negative pathways.

As children we are subjected to the behaviours of our parents day in and day out. We learn their beliefs and patterns of behaviour, and build neural pathways mimicking their behaviours. We also create neural pathways as coping mechanisms when we are upset by the behaviours of others that we experience as we are growing up. Some of these can be useful, for instance, becoming independent can be a great trait to have, as long as it doesn't result in you keeping people at a distance and having commitment issues.

Later in life these neural pathways can work against us by running patterns created by a trigger we stored many years ago. For example, Abby had a great childhood, but when her father got angry her mother would cry. Abby had learnt this behaviour and stored the trigger. When someone got angry near her she would break down in tears. Once the pattern was recognised and work was done on the original trigger, the pattern was altered. Instead she would feel acceptance and feel at ease. She had altered the neural pathway.

Transformational techniques work on these neural pathways by either breaking them, or giving them a positive slant, making them less intrusive in our lives. By putting in the time to work on ourselves in the same way we learnt to ride a bike, we can reprogram these patterns. We can become confident, happy, unstoppable, and at peace. We can then attract the many gifts that come with being in this happy state. As human beings we have great potential, especially when we are operating from a brain that is dominated by positive patterns. Life becomes easy.

For years we thought that the mind was a product of the brain. As the brain grew, we became more conscious and able to understand and grow further. This old paradigm has shifted and through research we now know that the brain is secondary to the mind. What is in our mind not only affects the structure of our brain, but also the cells in our bodies. It is no coincidence that the word disease spells dis-ease. When our minds are not at peace, our body is also in turmoil. When we understand and recognise that our minds are the controlling force that maps out our future, then we are able to use its power to transform not only our pathways, but our lives and the world around us.

I do not know everything there is to know about the science behind transformation process, however what I have come to learn through experience, research, and the thirst for knowledge, is a greater understanding of how our mind works and how we can be free from the constraints it imposes on us. My sole purpose and intentions in life, are to help people live happier lives. If this book makes a difference to just one person then my work here is done.

How Processes Saved My Life

In this book I am going to share with you the transformational processes I used to achieve happiness. I recommend that you use this workbook as a toolkit for your own transformation, and that you do all the processes listed herein.

First, I am going to tell you a little more about myself so that you can get an understanding of what I have broken through to become the person I am today. I am not saying I am perfect and free from all negative processes as we carry hundreds, but I am happier than I have ever been in my life, and have spent the last four years with a constant feeling of well-being and the belief that I can achieve anything.

As I said earlier, my childhood was lacking love. My father was also absent from about 2 years old. My father left when we were living in Zambia and my mother had to find a way to get us home with no money or passports. We eventually found a council provided house, in a poor suburb in a steel working town. My mother's father was leader of the council, therefore getting a house was fairly easy. Money however, was another matter. I remember my mother being frustrated and unhappy with us most of the time. I felt like a burden and often felt worthless to her. When I was about 5 my mother met a man that would cuddle and touch her affectionately. This intrigued me as I had never experienced this before. She became pregnant and gave birth to my little brother. From an early age my brother was ill, so even more attention was diverted from me. His father died from a brain haemorrhage about a year later. My brother's grandmother then spent much of his childhood buying him gifts and sweets. My sister and I often went without, leaving us feeling resentful.

Before my eighth birthday my mother met another guy that looked like was going to stick around. They married and we moved back to Zambia. There was a connection with the mine in the town we lived in and the mines in the copper belt in Zambia. My step-father was a violent man, not just in actions but also verbally. He was a bully and made me feel worthless almost daily. He called me "egghead". If I did something that was not to his liking I got thumped or slapped hard across the ear. We were not allowed to be children. Silence was his preference for us. A couple of years later he started sexually abusing me. It was only years later that I told my brother and he told me that the same thing happened to him. At 13 I got in to the wrong crowd and kept getting picked up by the police regularly for all sorts of misdemeanours. I was being bullied at school, but being a little tearaway gave me some purpose and identity.   By the time I left school I had been to 11 different schools. Eventually, my mother left my step-father and we moved in with my real Dad. I had requested to meet him and they had decided to try living together again. It didn't work and they split up after 3 months. I decided to stay with my father in Birmingham, as I resented my mother for the lack of care I had received. My father was not that great, but he did try initially. My father eventually asked me to leave home, as he didn't want me coming home drunk at night. By this time I was working in IT. It wasn't long before I was taking drugs. Weed to start with, but I moved on to hallucinogens.

By the time I was 19, I was lonely, depressed, anxious, and suicidal. I found it difficult to socialise and would make excuses not to be in situations I found difficult. When I was 21, I got married, had two children and then found myself divorced because I couldn't love my wife. I had no idea what love was or how to maintain a feeling of being loved. At 25 I started taking the recreational drug ecstasy and everything was great for a while, however the same old feeling and patterns kept coming up and were even intensified. I was in an intimate relationship, but I could feel myself constantly pushing her away or testing the relationship to see if she really wanted me. At 29 years old, I went to see an NLP practitioner and my life changed.   The shift was huge. After 3 sessions I was able to walk into a room without feeling like people were judging me. I was able to get on a bus, and not feel the need to sit at the back out of sight. I was able to look people in the eyes when I met them. I went from a shy guy hiding in the shadows, to a guy that wanted to experience life. This was just the beginning.

In case you don't know what an NLP practitioner is, then let me explain. It is an acronym for Neuro Linguistic Programming. It is a method of changing the neural pathways in the brain through the use of language. Using language you can guide someone's thoughts and change the way they think about something.   One of the techniques is called "re-framing" which had the most significant change on my life. I reframed

13 traumatic events in my childhood. Each time I left his therapy room, I was literally laughing. It is because of my positive experience with NLP, that I trained to become an NLP practitioner . I started researching and analysing everything I could in relation to myself and my relationships. I was even analysing other people's relationships. I could see things clearly for once and knew what I had to do to become anxiety and depression free.

I started doing courses and workshops that used transformational processes. I avoided the gimmicks and motivational seminars that just make you feel great for the time you are there, and then the feeling of elation soon fades. Motivational speaking only works for the time you are motivated. You can't stay motivated if the negative patterns are still firing and causing you to become misaligned with your true self. I tried lots of different types of therapy, but the only thing that worked was transformational processes that change the neural pathways that keep firing the negative patterns. Once you are at ease motivation comes easily. Your mind is no longer in turmoil. It stops racing at a million miles an hour.

 I remember I once wasted 4 hours in the back of a camper van going over the same thing again and again. I was not in control of the pattern. It was literally dominating my life. And this was just one pattern I could see. There were a lot that had subtle effects on me. They made me make choices that weren't the best for me. My ego was also getting out of control by this time, as I had some new confidence, but was still unaware of who I was. I carried on drinking and taking drugs as I went through courses and therapies looking for that elusive cure to my own worst enemy, my mind.

During my time in Australia I bought a book called the 'Handbook to Higher Consciousness,' by Ken Keyes Jr. It had a very intense dynamic transformational process in it. I found it difficult to maintain the thoughts and feelings for the length of time the process took, but I was intrigued. It got me thinking that there had to be an easier way.

I then met a yoga teacher in a club in London who told me about the Hoffman Process. The process is an intensive week-long residential course that uses transformational processes. I knew I had to do it. I called them and booked myself on the course. At the time the course was about £2500. Today the course is around £3000.

The price puts it out of reach for a large part of the population, not to mention the one week of holiday you would need to take if you were in full-time employment.

I was lucky enough to be working in London at the time in a well paid job, so I decided to do it.

As the course unfolded, I was aware that the processes were transformational in their nature and that they were having a very profound effect on me. Each day I felt a little different, as another pattern was broken. I was also aware of the techniques being used to strengthen my identity and mind in the event of future upsets that could have me going way off the rails again. I spent the next year bounding around in life, feeling like a totally different person. I researched what I had learnt and looked at what I could do to further my progress, as I knew that courses alone would not be the solution to finding true peace.

Later that year I did a series of courses by Landmark Education, that also uses transformational processes. They are delivered in a different manner to the Hoffman Process and although not as powerful, it still had a profound effect on me. There is something totally different about a course that has 90 participants that are all trying to break through their negative patterns, compared to an intimate course with just 12 people. The Landmark courses gave me more insight into what processes worked best.

There are thousands of people around the globe using the power of their minds to heal their past and even to heal their own bodies. Some people have literally healed serious back injuries through the power of thought. This can also be seen in the placebo effect. When a patient believes they are getting better, their health improves so much that statistically it's no coincidence. This has been tested on thousands of patients.

What we lack is the self-belief that we can actually heal our past with our mind. This is why transformational processes are so powerful. They give us faith in a process. The process in its nature is powerful enough to make changes to our neural pathways and even create new ones, but trusting in the process furthers our ability to heal. A shining example is the use of affirmations. Repeating positive phrases may at first be difficult and the person repeating them often finds it hard to believe them, but eventually they sink into the subconscious mind. After some time of repeating the phrases they don't seem so ridiculous and they settle with you easily. By this point new neural pathways are in place and being strengthened.

This is why I am delivering these processes in workbook form. This is a journey that is best done alone and at your own pace, but with repetition. It is essential that you participate 100% in your transformation process. You should complete each process fully in order to get the full benefit. That is not to say that doing just one process won't have an effect. If you want to be the best you can be in life and live to your full potential then you owe it to yourself to commit 100%.

The primary reason that individuals stay mired in their unhappy lives is because they don't know how to utilise the processes that will create a better life for themselves. Although it sounds very obvious, this creates a major roadblock for most individuals today. Complaining about how miserable your life is never rectifies the situation. Dreaming about a better life, won't help you achieve that either.

Whether you attend seminars, exchange personal ideas, read books that are inspirational, or talk with other people, it still won't help you to achieve your goals of living a better life. We have all looked for a quick fix at some point in our lives, even though we don't believe in them or trust that someone is selling one that truly works.

This is exactly why we avoid getting involved in some types of program that could help us achieve these things. Creating a better life for oneself is very challenging, and that is exactly why we shy away from making an attempt at doing it. It is also the exact reason why a structured program can help you. There is a lot of work ahead of you, don't kid yourself. However, all the hand, head, heart, and foot work that you will encounter is going to be beneficial in the long run. This workbook is specifically designed with your everyday life in mind, and is guaranteed to have a profound and lasting effect on you. You will be happier, I can assure you of that.

These days I find it hard to find something negative to think about. I am happy, have no anxiety, and I am no longer depressed. I enjoy meeting new people without the social anxiety that dogged me for years. I am able to enter new relationships and work out quickly whether they are the right one for me. I now focus on creating a life for myself where I can earn enough money to be happy, whilst also helping other people.

Who Are You?

Before we go into the processes, I am going to talk about our identity and why it is important to know who we are and what we stand for. Without a clear idea of who we really are, we are creating incongruence with our identity and our false self. If we are challenged we will not feel grounded in our identity and will be unable to speak from the heart. We will be defensive rather than relaxed and confident. If you have had someone challenge your point of view and you felt like they were attacking you, then there is a good chance that you were not rooted in your identity. You were unclear about who you are and why you have that point of view. This is because for years we can hide behind a mask, a false image of ourselves that we created from an early age to avoid being hurt. This is not the real you, the real you is screaming to get out but is too scared to do so without the support it needs. Only when we are living authentically from our true identity can we feel grounded and operate with integrity.

Logical Levels of Change

The "Logical levels of Change" model is a valuable road map for seeing a clear picture of how our identity affects our lives. Making a change to one of the levels will affect the level below, which in turn supports the level above. It is for this reason we start at the top of the pyramid and work down. I include these within this workbook as an insight to who we are at present and what we can do to effectively create our new selves.

The levels are:

1.   Mission/Vision/Purpose

2.   Identity

3.   Values & Beliefs

4.   Capabilities & Skills

5.   Behaviour

6.   Environment

Figure 3 - Logical Levels of Change Model

1 – Mission, Vision, Purpose

This level is related to your spirituality and ultimately finding what your purpose is in life. If you have no idea what your purpose is, then this may have an effect on who you are being. Studies have shown that the happiest people in life are those that have found their purpose. For some this may mean owning a house, raising a family, and then looking after grandchildren. For some people it is that simple. But as family values are becoming more and more diluted, many people are lost and feel they have no purpose. This is why we must create a purpose based on who we are and what we want out of life.

For example, Debbie a nurse at a general hospital chose her purpose based on how she felt about people and her desire to help those that were ill or unable to cope. Many people also have jobs that do not fit their purpose in life. John for instance became an accountant, pushed into it by his father and his family's expectations. It wasn't until John was 35 that he had the insight that led him to change his career and become a manager for the Forestry Commission. John was always drawn to nature and he felt his purpose was to make a difference in that area.

Finding your purpose may not be that easy, but the best place to start is to think about what it is you would really like to make a difference to. Maybe it is a community, or a certain set of people, maybe it is animals and saving their environments, or perhaps you are interested in collecting historical items for the worlds archives.

Having a purpose may not mean having a particular career. It might simply be who you are in life and what you stand for. Being a caring and giving person in whatever life you are blessed with, may be purpose enough for you to feel fulfilled.

You may just have a vision of what you want for the future and are working towards that. Having a large goal that is bigger than yourself creates a purpose in your life.

According to Carl Yung, we are all one of sixteen personality types. He devised a test of 72 questions that will accurately show you what personality type you are and what career you

are best suited. You can take the test here:
http://www.humanmetrics.com/cgi-win/JTypes2.asp

2 – Identity

The identity can best be described as who you see yourself to be. Who are you in life? What do you stand for? Do you have personal integrity? Your mission/vision/purpose plays a huge part in your identity. As does the level below identity, your values and beliefs. Do you have a set of beliefs and values and stick to them no matter what?

As children we do many things to change our identity including wearing certain types of clothes in order to fit in. Without a fixed identity we have less self-esteem.

For instance, I had a set of values for years but on occasion my behaviour would go against them. My identity would be weakened and I would lose self-esteem. To counteract this I would self-medicate usually with alcohol, which incidentally was the reason my behaviour went awry in the first place.

3 – Beliefs and Values

We learn some of our beliefs and values from an early age and this is usually from our parents. When we experience something we really don't like, we usually create an inverse belief, one that is the total opposite of the one we experienced. When I was a child I felt very uncared for, so I developed a part of myself that reaches out to people in need.

When we experience something that we really like then we want to be that way too, and therefore some of our more positive values are created.

Our parents, teachers, and peers all have an effect on our belief system. Whether this is our superstitions, the God we do or don't follow, whether we reincarnate, or whether this is all a dream, to name a few. It is important to get these clear in order to give our identity some stability.

Values and beliefs can change through life as we learn and grow.

If you grew up in a dysfunctional family, you may have a set of self-limiting beliefs. You may believe that you are not good enough, or that you are unlovable or not liked. These are all easily transformed.

4 – Capabilities & Skills

Once you have reassessed your values and beliefs, you can start to make the necessary changes to your capabilities. What skills and capabilities do you currently have? Are they helping you affect change in the areas of your life that you want to make a difference? Maybe you need to start thinking about new skills. For example, learning how to teach, learning a language, or learning IT. Skills and capabilities will open new doors for you. This may mean many hours of work. For instance, one of the things that I value and I am inspired by is playing the guitar. Therefore, I play the guitar every week in order to better myself. I have also taken meditation courses because I know the value of learning this skill. Increasing your skill set can only have a good effect on your life.

5 – Behaviour

Behaviour is not just what you do, but also how you think and feel. This is why the previous stages are so important, as our actions are usually dictated by how we feel.

Have you ever noticed how you have behaved after the event has actually happened? That is because your patterns of behaviour already took you down the familiar path you so easily went many times before. If you could stop for just a second and observe how you feel before that pattern kicks in, you will be able to make a choice. Do I behave this way, or do I recognise that this is just a response to how I am feeling? Meditation is one of the most powerful tools for bringing awareness to our feelings. It would benefit you to make one of your new skills the ability to meditate. It will pay untold dividends and is why millions of people meditate every day.

6 – Environment

Take a look at your life. What does it look like? What have you achieved? Where are you going? Who are your friends? Are you where you want to be?

We can't create our environment authentically, without first having the other stages in sync.

Don't be too hung up on the path you took to get you to this stage. Think instead of the new path that you are going to create for yourself. The path you took was the "You" that was not as aware as you are today. You were running on a set of patterns invoked by feelings that created actions, that thus created your current environment.

When I realised the environment I was in was not in line with my true values, I changed my environment. I moved out of the city, retrained, and started working from home. I then had a lot more time to do the things that really mattered to me.

From the Logical Levels of Change model, we can work out what levels we would like to change and what levels really need to change. Take some time to think about this and to think about who you really want to be in life.

Areas of Life

When you start to look at your life for the first time you may feel overwhelmed and not find it easy to see where exactly your life isn't in balance. The best way to progress is to write down all the different areas of your life and then look at those individually to see if there is any upset, stress, or imbalance there. The following are some areas of life that may be relevant to you. Feel free to add your own.

- Home
- Family
- Physical Health
- Mental Health
- Work
- Career
- Hobbies/Free time
- Finances
- Friends
- Relationships
- Sex
- Education
- Spirituality

When you have pinpointed a key area that is not going smoothly, look at what you could do to change that area. It might mean looking for a new job, letting go of some toxic friends, or ending an intimate relationship. As long the problem isn't coming from you and you don't feel there is anything you could change in yourself to make it better, then sometimes we have to change what is outside of us. We will come across negative people and situations throughout our lives. It is up to us whether we choose to have that negativity in our lives. Negativity impedes our growth and can hold us back from our dreams.

Exercise: Key areas of Life

Write down all the key areas of your life where you are unhappy or stressed.

- Home
- Family
- Physical Health
- Mental Health
- Work
- Career
- Hobbies/Free time
- Finances
- Friends
- Relationships
- Sex
- Education
- Spirituality

What can you do for each of the areas you wrote down to make it better? Do you need a job change? A new career? Do you need to end a relationship? Do you need to drink less? Do you need to eat healthier? Whatever it may be, just be aware of it for now.

Building Self Esteem and Confidence

Your self-esteem is your overall self-value and self-worth. This is created from a very early age. If you lived in a very loving home, were encouraged and your failures were backed up with positivity, then you are likely to have high self-esteem.

If you did not feel loved or adequately cared for or one of your parents rejected you, then your self-esteem may be low. Your self-esteem was created over many years of input from the people and environment around you. Your neural pathways are literally programmed over time. If you have low self-esteem this could mean you didn't build the positive neural pathways as a child, to give you the confidence to do anything without the fear of failing.

One of the key aspects regarding personal growth is learning how to gain (or regain) one's self-confidence. Along with our self-esteem, nothing in our lives encounters more "knocks" than our self-confidence. Unfortunately, most of us are unaware of the fact that we need to reassess our levels of self-confidence and continually work on rebuilding them. Additionally, the many situations in life that we deal with on a day-to-day basis are affected by our level of self-confidence.

Interestingly enough, we may be confident in the interpersonal relationships we encounter in our social lives, but lack confidence in our career environment (and vice-versa). It is obvious then, that when you work on your self-confidence, you need to work on it from all angles, not just in one specific area.

The lack of self-confidence can originate from a variety of sources. These include:

- Bad situations in your life that haven't been addressed or dealt with in a proper fashion

- Influences from parental and peer figures

- Past childhood experiences

The Hard and Fast Rule about Self-Confidence

Gaining self-confidence comes from building self-confidence – pure and simple. And the only hope we have of doing this comes from the ability to build new neural pathways. Self-appreciation is another one of the key concepts that you can employ in order to accomplish this. Self-discovery and self-inventory are key ways in which you get to know the true person that you are, in order to be able to value yourself. It not only helps to improve the confidence you have in yourself, it is also the most ideal way to improve your self-esteem and self-worth.

3 Initial Steps to Improving Self-Confidence

Although there are many schools of thought regarding the improvement of self-confidence, the following are the 3 initial steps that you need to take in order to get on the right track:

1 – Identity.

We already looked at this in the Logical Levels of Change model. By creating a solid identity we have already started to build our self-confidence. Most individuals today set out to build or rebuild their self-confidence without placing value on themselves. You need to be aware of your best qualities by knowing who you truly are as a human being.

If you are unsure what it is that you admire and like about yourself, then take the time to reflect on the positive qualities of what you feel you are all about.

Exercise: Increasing Self Confidence

Ask yourself the following 3 questions:

1.   What do you consider to be your greatest strengths and weaknesses?

2.   What is it that makes you so good at certain things, whilst you cannot succeed at others?

3.   What makes you a unique individual?

Make a handwritten list of these questions, carry it around with you, and read it every day for the next 30 days. This is the first thing that you need to do in order to start building or rebuilding your self-confidence.

You cannot start working on your self-confidence if you are constantly thinking negatively about yourself. The most common mistake we make is that we continually compare ourselves to other individuals. This is very destructive and results in constantly putting yourself down. People are attracted to one another based on the levels of self-confidence of the other person, as well as being passionate about their lives and what they are doing. It inspires those around you. Besides that, when you continually display or voice a negative opinion about yourself, you will make those around you feel uncomfortable in your presence.

Credit must be given to Louise Hay whose book, 'You Can Heal Your Life' has transformed the lives of millions of people. She learnt the power of affirmations and shared it with the world. Affirmations have got me out of a dark place on many occasions. We are very good at storing negative thoughts, most of which are fabricated by our inability to see the reality. For instance, a parent shouting at their child telling them that they are useless will have a long-term negative effect. Just that small seed of doubt is enough to affect your decisions and well-being later in life. By creating positive messages and repeating them again and again we are able to reprogram the negative areas.

The single most powerful affirmation I have found is, "I love and accept myself." I had a bout of anxiety years ago that wouldn't leave me, so I sat down and said this affirmation for about 10 minutes after which time my anxiety disappeared.

You can make your own affirmations to suit whatever negativity you find.

I love and accept myself

I am worthy and loveable

I am a strong loving person

Process: Affirmations

Choose an affirmation. Find a comfortable place where you won't be disturbed or go for a walk where you can be alone.

Repeat your affirmation. You will eventually find a rhythm as the words leave your mouth and you take a breath of air. You may wish to repeat it 3 times before taking that breath.

Be sure to put some emotion behind what you are saying. You may not necessarily believe it at the moment, but you are planting a seed and this will grow over time. As the saying goes, fake it till you make it. If it doesn't sound true pretend it is true. Be the actor in a play and say with emotion, "I Love and Accept Myself".

3 – Positivity

Surround yourself with positive individuals that will influence you in a more positive fashion. It's like the old adage – if you want to be successful, surround yourself with successful people. To illustrate what we are talking about here, take the time to observe the behaviour of confident and positive individuals around you when in a social setting. I'm not telling you to copy these individuals, but emulating them is another story. You're simply taking on the characteristics of these individuals in order to enhance your personal portfolio and increase your positivity levels.

Additionally, you need to commit and dedicate yourself to building your self-confidence level. Work on employing those thoughts that are inspiring and uplifting, not self-defeating. Diving into a book about the lives of inspirational individuals is a great way to get started in this area. Carefully look at how they have got the things they want out of life by overcoming certain obstacles in their lives that initially prevented them from achieving or attaining these things.

Most importantly . . .

Get started on an unstoppable mission to build your self-confidence!

Process – Meeting Yourself

For some people this can be a very difficult process and for others it is a breeze. The reason we do this is to see if there is a disconnection from our true selves. If you find this process uncomfortable, then there is a good chance that there are parts of yourself that you do not like and that you do not want to accept as being part of you. Only when we can accept ourselves fully, can we fully love ourselves and thus gain greater self-worth.

Follow the instructions below.

1. Sit in front of a mirror no more than a metre away so that you can see the whole of your face clearly.

2. Look into your eyes.

3. Be aware of any discomfort or agitation in your thoughts.

4. Note what you are thinking about yourself as you look at your face.

5. Speak to yourself by saying "Hello, {your name}. I just wanted to let you know that I love you".

6. Do you believe your own words?

7. Record on a scale from one to ten how uncomfortable the process was with ten being the most uncomfortable. Keep this written somewhere, as we will need it later.

Actions such as the above will enable you to hit the ground running, to start building your self-confidence and create the type of person that everyone wants to be in the presence of. One day people will be asking you, why you're so happy and how you got to be the way you are.

"You've been walking in circles, searching. Don't drink by the water's edge. Throw yourself in. Become the water. Only then will your thirst end." -- Jeanette Berson

Mindfulness and the Ego

Mindfulness is the practice of paying attention to the present by observing your thoughts, feelings, and actions. This powerful in the "now" experience gives us a chance to become aware of our negative patterns that have led us to a lifetime of suffering. By becoming more aware of our thoughts and feelings we can change those things within us that cause us suffering.

Do you ever find yourself getting angry or upset at what people say? Have you ever got angry at another driver? Do certain people always seem to rub you up the wrong way?

Being aware of your feelings, thoughts, actions, and patterns of behaviour does not come naturally. If it did the world would be a different place. Practising observing our thoughts and emotions and seeing what they are driving us to say and do is very useful in breaking our negative behaviour.

Once we are recognising negative patterns, we can act differently by acknowledging the old pattern and creating a new one.

I spoke earlier about our identity and how it is based on the creation of our values and beliefs. It is this identity that brought about our ego. The ego is counterproductive and is a construction of our false-self based on our external world. It focuses more on our abilities, how we look, what we think other people think of us, how much prestige we have, and how good we are. It is only interested in 'I' or 'Me'.

It is preoccupied with the lower centres of consciousness; security, sensation and power. It is responsible for triggering those negative patterns that seem to plague us. Think of it as the control room for all your negative patterns. It is trying to protect you from fear that you felt previously. It makes us do things that are not our true selves.

Some people are obsessed with their bodies, forever in the gym, either toning or getting huge in order to counteract their self-esteem. Others are preoccupied with other people's problems and become judgemental, again to offset how they feel about themselves.

If someone bumps into you and doesn't say sorry then your ego may take offence and you become angry at that person. Who knows why they didn't say sorry, it is not our problem, the only thing we can do is become aware of what our ego did to us. It is never the force outside of ourselves that hurts us, it is our ego's reaction to that force.   Being offended is just our inability to deal with the emotions that arise in the moment.

Exercise: Mindfulness

Practice keeping a mental note every time someone dents your ego. Also look at what pattern was triggered. It might take a while to recognise the pattern, but keep observing. Try to understand what your ego wanted to happen in that situation and what outcome would have made it OK. Then realise that there is nothing that should happen to make it OK, only our reaction to that situation can make it OK. Next time you get angry at someone, say to yourself, "I am the one getting angry at myself". Smile inside knowing that you are in control.

Process: Mindfulness

The following process is a great way of reminding us that the negative pattern that we are currently in is not serving us. The thing with most patterns is that they are satisfying our ego. We must remind our ego that this is not what it needs right now.

Process – Short Sharp Shock

Wear an elastic band on your wrist.

As soon as you recognise a pattern of behaviour that isn't serving you pull the elastic band and let it snap against your wrist so that it hurts. Then say, "That's not me, I am not this pattern."

Repeat this process every time the pattern comes up.

When you are in a negative pattern you are acting from neural pathways that make you feel most comfortable once you have been triggered. By causing yourself a short sharp shock you are creating new neural pathways that are telling you that this negative pattern causes you pain. The more you repeat this process, the less likely you are to activate the pattern again.

Positivity

Whether you think you can or think you can't, you are right. You brain is a computer and what you put into it will come out. What you feel right now is what you are going to attract into your life. If you live in doubt and question everything, then your life is going to be one fraught with difficult decisions. If you live with a positive attitude and believe that whatever happens is just part of a bigger picture, then your life will flow. I learnt this story many years ago and I often tell it to people that feel that they have hit the bottom.

A man fell into a fast flowing river and was washed away. The king was passing with his men and saw what happened, so they raced after him. Occasionally they would see his head come back to the surface, as he was spun through the rapids and most of the time he was under the water. Eventually the man was regurgitated from the white water and crawled up a bank, where the king's men raced to meet him. The king enquired as to how on he had survived such a torrid river. He replied, "The River is like the force of life. There is little you can do to change what is happening in the present. When it takes you down, do not struggle as this is a waste of energy. Let the river take you. When you come back up, take a breath and be grateful. Know that this will pass and you will soon be walking through life again as if it had never happened."

When you replace negative thoughts with positive ones, you will start living a positive life. By adapting a positive mind over a set period of time you are changing the neural pathways that were once pointing in a negative direction and moving them into a positive direction. Once you have changed the neural pathways you will actually feel more alive, positive, and happier.

Process: Positivity – See the good in all things

The next time you leave the house and go somewhere, have a positive attitude about everything. When you see a homeless man, see it as part of his journey. Give him something to help him on that journey. When you see people arguing, see this as their egos clashing and understand that it is part of their journey. See the beauty in the things around you. Whether you are in a city or in the countryside, smile and think about how positive your day is going to be. If the person you are meeting is late or whether the bus is late use that extra time you have to think about the things that are important to you.

When you experience negative thoughts about yourself catch them and turn them around. Find the positive in the subject you are thinking about.

You may experience the negativity coming back again, but keep seeing positive in all things. Make this a daily practice.

Gratitude

Gratitude is a very powerful emotion that gives us the realisation of how amazing our lives actually are. By practising gratitude, especially when you are down, can give you that boost you need to get you back on track. No matter how down you are, there is always something to be grateful for. It is also a great tool for bringing you back into the present moment, which I will cover in the next process. Practice gratitude for just a few minutes every day or a couple of times a week.

"Gratitude unlocks the fullness of life. It turns what we have into enough, and more. It turns denial into acceptance, chaos to order, confusion to clarity. It can turn a meal into a feast, a house into a home, a stranger into a friend." -- Melody Beattie

Here are 7 scientifically proven benefits of Gratitude

1. Improves physical health

2. Improves mental health

3. Leads to more relationships

4. Reduces aggression and increases empathy

5. Improves sleep

6. Improves Self-esteem

7. Improves mental strength

Process: Gratitude

Write down 10 things that you are grateful for right now.

Find something to be grateful for every day as you wake up and write it down in a notepad next to your bed. At the end of the week review what you have written, turn the page and start a new one.

Friends

Choosing the right friends is difficult, especially as we met most of our friends when we were less aware of who we were and what our values were. As we continue to grow, we find that some friends are great for our self-esteem, they care and nurture us and listen to our opinions. Others however can be the opposite and can drain us of our energy with their negativity. Sometimes we are able to assist others in finding a better path, but some people are just not interested in creating a better life for themselves. It is better to let these friends go or at least limit the amount of time you spend with them.

Exercise: Friends that Appreciate You

Write down the friends that value and respect you. These are the friends that you should be spending more time with. If you are struggling to think of any friends that are this way with you, then maybe it is time to join some meet up groups and make new friends. Use the Meetup.com website to find people with the same interests. Take up dancing or some other group learning class.

The Past

When we talk about the past, we are talking about something that no longer exists, yet for us it is still very real. Why is this? Why does the past have such an impact on our lives? Everything that happens we take on through our filter of the world and subconsciously rank it in terms of how much it affected us.

There is a part of the brain known as the limbic system that records memories of events and the impact they have on us. In our lives this part of the brain tells us whether we should avoid the situation. Now this was great when we were roaming around avoiding other tribes and avoiding poisonous food. When we entered an unknown region and our limbic system recognised it as being similar to the place we were last attacked, it would raise our adrenalin and put us in a heightened state, so that we were ready to deal with whatever was ahead of us. The only problem with this is that it also stores emotional pain. This is the part that ignites the ego. If your childhood sweetheart ends your relationship and you are left devastated, you may feel anxious when you are in a relationship again (in the future) because you are anxious that they are going to leave you.

Life is full of upset and unless we are able to deal with it right there in that moment, then we will be storing a negative response to the situation. There is a lot of work that we must do with our past in order to resolve it. Each incident is its own book with its own story. In order to be free from the effects that it has on our present we must rewrite the end of the book, close it, and let go of the past.

Regret is a negative emotion based on a person's past actions or behaviours. The actions of the past cannot be changed, although amends can be made in the present if you wish to get closure on something you did in the past. Getting closure on past wrongdoings is a very powerful way to let go of the past and create or reaffirm your own moral code. We cover this in some later processes.

Process: The Past

Think of a time in the past when you felt upset. Now with that feeling still present within you, think of another time previous to that. Keep doing this process until you are able to think way back to when you were much younger and you had this feeling. Write down this incident in detail. What were you doing? Where were you? Who was there? What caused the upset?

Do this with as many feelings of upset as you can. Take each feeling back as far as you can and write down the incident.   Also write down the names of the people that you feel were the cause of your upset.

You can do this process at night before you go to sleep. Being in a relaxed state will help you recall the past events. We will be using these incidents from the past in a process later in this workbook.

The Present

The present is all that exists. You can only experience it one second at a time. You can create stuff in the present that can change the coming present moments, but ultimately the present is the only thing you cannot change as it is already happening. This is useful to know when life is kicking you when you are down. This is an adaption of a story I read in a Ken Keyes book.

A man was trekking in a great mountain forest. It was raining heavily and he came to a clearing on the side of a cliff. Suddenly there was a flash flood and he was washed over the edge. He managed to grab a vine as he fell. Below him was a huge drop that only had one outcome should he fall. He looked up and could see that the vine was no longer connected to the tree, but was part wrapped around a branch and was slowly unravelling. It was only seconds before he would fall. In that moment he looked around and saw the beauty of the mountain, the trees, the river and valley below. He smelled the beauty of the forest. Before him on the side of the cliff was a small bush with edible berries. He picked a berry and ate it and tasted it with such passion. As he fell he heard, saw and felt everything possible.

Practice being in the present moment wherever you are. Get out of your head, look around, see everything, hear everything and feel everything. Also bring gratitude to this moment.

The Future

The future does not exist, but is an imagination created by our mind that is in the present moment. We can shape the future by actions in the now. When we are worrying about something, we are in the imagined future. We are creating a picture of the future usually based on some fear from the past. Bring yourself back to the present moment. Breathe and be aware of the present moment. Ask yourself, what in this moment is lacking? Think about it for a while. This will bring you back to the present moment, as there is no past or present in this moment. If you have an answer then you have either gone into the past or present to find that answer.

Unlike other animals we humans have a level of intelligence that allows us to create anything we want. Then why is it that most of us go through a cycle of work, play, work, play, work, without creating what we really want in life. We are conditioned to believe that the most important thing in life is to find a job, get a house, get a partner, have children, etc. You don't have to do any of those things to be happy. Ask yourself this question, "If you never had to work again and could be anywhere in the world, what would you want to be doing with your life?" Be sure to choose something that you want to be doing for the next 10 years. Sitting on a beach sipping cocktails would become a bit monotonous after a couple of years.

The future that you create for yourself will actually make you happy because you chose it. It doesn't have to be reality right now. For instance, you can create a 5 year plan to build your dream home on the side of a mountain where you will live growing your own vegetables and foraging from the forest. You could spend the first year researching, becoming inspired, planning, etc. The next four years you could be in action to make your dream come true. I'm not saying it is going to be an easy journey, but it will definitely be worth it.

"If you can't believe in miracles, then believe in yourself. When you want something bad enough, let that drive push you to make it happen. Sometimes you'll run into brick walls that are put there to test you. Find a way around them and stay focused on your dream. Where there's a will, there's a way." -- Isabel Lopez

People who have a set plan for their future are happier people. They are living into a future that they are creating for themselves. This is the first level of the Logical Levels of Change. Your vision.

Anger

Anger is one of the most destructive emotions we know. It does not just affect the mind, but has also been proven to have a negative impact on our bodies and our health. The latest research has shown that anger can weaken the immune system and be a gateway for the onset of disease. Further studies from Washington State University found that people who express their anger by lashing out, are at a higher risk of heart attack due to an increase in calcium deposits in their coronary arteries.

The Centres for Disease Control and Prevention state that 85% of all diseases appear to have an emotional element and that the figure is probably much higher.

There are many ways to channel and resolve anger using techniques and practices like NLP, EFT, hypnotherapy, cathartic release, etc. We will be using the cathartic release process, because of its effectiveness at releasing anger.

People who release and resolve their anger are known to have better relationships, happier lives, and a better connection with themselves and the world they live in.

Anger is known to be so dense that it traps the feelings of upset below it. By releasing anger we are able to release the trapped negative emotions that have been within us for years.

Earlier in this workbook you wrote down the names of some of the people that upset you. If you can think of any other people that have upset you in the past, then add them to this list.

For each of the people that caused you to be upset, you are now going to express your anger towards them.   Even if you no longer feel angry towards them it is important that you go through this process. We cope with emotions by blocking them out, by burying them deep within us. In this process people often find that they had no idea they held any anger for the person whom they were focussing. Even if you find it difficult to get angry it works to at first pretend to feel angry. "Fake it till you Make it" is the old adage. Using words you would use when angry shout as loud as you can as if the person was standing in front of you. You will need some privacy to do this. Some people do this while in the car, or maybe you can walk in a remote location. Another method would be to scream into a pillow. You can also do it under water. This version of the process has been the most effective for me, but feel free to adapt it to fit your surroundings. Once you have completed your five minutes you may find that you feel upset or like crying. This is normal. The real pain sits below the anger.

Process: Releasing Anger

Before doing this process be sure to read the next chapter about Forgiveness. This is the really rewire the neural pathways and give you much peace.

Find a private place, say a bedroom. Put on some loud music. Kneel on the bed with a pillow in front of you. Choose one of the people that upset you in the past.

Tense your body as much as you can. Now start hitting the pillow with your fists. Scream at the person as if they were in front of you. Tell them how much they hurt you. Tell them how much you hate them. Curse and swear if you need to. Keep doing this for this person for at least 5 whole minutes. Keep hitting the pillow. Cry if you need to.

After you have completed this process, it is important that you read the next chapter on Forgiveness and complete the processes within.

Forgiveness

Often forgiveness is linked to anger, which is why we work with these side by side. By empathising with the focus on your anger, you are able to release this negative energy and open a path to full resolution. Using guided meditations you can be taken on a journey where you are able to forgive at a deep level. People who forgive in this way indicate that it is like saying goodbye to a darker side of themselves. Forgiveness is more about you than the person you are forgiving. Remember also to forgive yourself. You are a human with a set of programs that were created during your past that you had no control over. Your past actions are just a result of this programming.

The following process is used for forgiving others. It is a guided meditation. Read the instructions carefully and memorise them. Then do the process. It is better that you know the process, as you will be relaxed with your eyes closed.

Process: Forgiving Others

Find a place where you won't be disturbed. This process will take about 15 minutes. Learn the whole process before starting it.

Close your eyes. I want you to imagine that you are walking across the lawn of large house. It is a warm summer's day and a cooling breeze flows around you. The lawn stretches out far behind the house and as you walk away from the house, you begin to see some steps leading down to a rose garden. You can smell the roses as you reach the steps. Now I want you to think of one of the people that upset you.

Start descending the steps one by one. With each step you take, you feel more and more relaxed. With each step you take you go deeper and deeper into relaxation. Descend the seven steps one by one slowly, each time feeling more and more relaxed.

When you get to the bottom of the steps you walk through the rose garden, observing the roses and smells as you go. There is a little trail that leads down to a small river. You take the trail. You see a large tree beside the river.   Underneath the tree you can see a small child sitting on a log.   As you approach the child you see that it is the person that upset you as a child. They are crying. You ask why they are crying. They tell you that it is because they are finding things difficult and that they are scared. You comfort them and tell them things will be OK. Ask them what their life is like as a child. Listen to what words come to you as you feel and empathise with them.   In this moment you realise that when they grow up they will still have these feelings and that these feelings were probably the cause of them upsetting you.   You reach deep into your heart and forgive them for they are just as frightened as you. You put your arms around this small frightened child and hug them. They stop crying and you release them.

You wave goodbye and wish them all the best. Return to the rose garden and open your eyes when you are ready.

You must repeat this process for each person you got angry at. You can do the next process after each of the people you chose for the previous process.

Process: Letter of Forgiveness

Find a private place to write a letter. Following on from the above process, write a letter to the adult version of the person that upset you.

Write down all your thoughts and feelings towards this person. Tell them how you feel inside now, how you felt before. Don't write anything that is an expectation of them. In other words don't ask them to say sorry, as that is not their job.

When you have completed the letter save it somewhere safe as we will be doing a fire cleanse ritual later in the workbook.

Guilt

Guilt is another one of the top destructive emotions. People carry it around with them for years without dealing with it. Most guilt should not even exist as it is an emotion that is born from your own moral standards. A lot of moral standards are created by other people when we were growing up. For example, a lady was unhappy in her marriage, but had tremendous guilt that she didn't love her husband and wanted to leave him. They were both unhappy because of a standard that had been created by her parents and their conversations about how a marriage is for life. Once this lady saw that she hadn't created this standard for herself and that she didn't actually believe it, the guilt left her and she was able to tell her husband how she felt and they separated amicably and are now both happy in their own lives.

Some people feel guilty because of the way they acted in the past. As long as you are not that same person, then there is nothing to feel guilty about. You were acting from a set of patterns, values and beliefs of a younger more immature version of who you are now. Forgive yourself and realise that if you were in that same situation again and knowing what you know now, that you wouldn't act that way. You're off the hook. You were growing and learning.

Exercise – Guilt

1.   Write down anything you feel guilty about.

2.   Forgive yourself for being human and remind yourself that you are becoming a better person.

3.   If there is someone you wronged, then make a note of them as we will use them in a later process.

Health and Diet

Studies have shown that what you eat can have a direct impact on your mood. Fruit and vegetables contain essential vitamins and minerals that are known to keep us chemically balanced. If we eat a diet without these essential vitamins and minerals then the impact on our mood can be quite damaging to our mental health. Your sleep can also be affected by your diet. Your ability to rationalise or deal with negative thoughts becomes more difficult and this can pull you down further. Keeping hydrated is also important to keeping us in a healthy place.

In order to grow new neural pathways, our bodies need the nutrients essential in brain development. You should supply your brain with nutrients that improve brain plasticity such as polyphenols, flavonols, and omega-3 essential fatty acids.

Luckily polyphenols are abundant in the typical diet. However, the following foods contain high levels; cloves, star anise, cocoa powder, celery seed, black chokeberry, dark chocolate, flaxseed meal, black elderberry, and chestnut.

Flavonols are also abundant in a typical diet, but to increase your intake try eating; onions, apples, romaine lettuce, tomatoes, garbanzo beans, almonds, turnip greens, sweet potatoes, and quinoa.

Omega-3 is usually associated with fish, but our fish is mostly contaminated with heavy metals these days, which seriously affects brain development. I would recommend these sources; walnuts, chia seeds, flax seeds, algae and hemp.

Doing regular exercise is equally as important as eating correctly. Even if you can only manage a short walk each day, getting the blood flowing through your body and moving the joints and muscles will release chemicals in the brain that are known to increase your mood and put you in a good state of mind. Also a healthy body will make you feel better about yourself. If you are out of shape, put a six month plan together to get fitter. Join a class like Yoga or Pilates. Or maybe even a dance class.

"Better keep yourself clean and bright; you are the window through which you must see the world" -- George Bernard Shaw

Attachment

Attachment is the process by which we put importance on certain objects or outcomes. It is created by our desire to attain something, which in turn makes us feel good. Somewhere in the past we created neural pathways to things that we thought were very important. When we don't get these things then we are not firing those neural pathways, which release the chemicals that cause us to be happy. With attachment we are creating expectations. For example, when we call a loved one that we really want to speak to, we are attached to an expectation. We want them to be on the other end of the phone. We are expecting them to pick up. When they don't answer this causes our ego to fire another set of neural pathways that cause us fear and doubt.

By becoming aware of our attachments we can program ourselves to accept that our expectations might not always be met. This is a powerful practice and can literally take the sting out of not getting what we want. Our expectations then become preferences. When something is a preference, we are less likely to become upset when things do not go our way.

Exercise: Attachment

Write down 10 items you are attached to.

Write down 10 outcomes you are attached to.

A great practice in becoming less attached to material things, is to have a declutter. Take all the things you don't use anymore to the charity shop or have a yard sale. At first this may seem a bit daunting. The thoughts going through your mind might be, "I might need it one day," "It means a lot to me," or "It's a part of my past." These are all valid thoughts, but in reality you can't take them with you beyond this life so what value do they really have.

People that get rid of their clutter report that it felt like a huge relief. Some say it was like they threw a lot of negativity away with the items. There are also the obvious benefits like more space and a tidier home.

Process: Attachment de-clutter

Each week get rid of one or more items.

Letting Go

Letting go can refer to letting go of what we are holding onto that we think is stopping us from feeling fear. It can also refer to identifying and holding on to the pain that we have experienced. It is believed that pain can be become entwined with our identity and we know any changes to the identity can be a scary prospect.

When something traumatic happens to us, we swallow all that pain far down into our tissue fibres and then carry on like nothing had happened, or at least until something triggers the stored pain again. When animals experience trauma they shake. Some even find a quiet place to shake out all the negative energy without being disturbed. It is no wonder we carry our emotional pain around with us like a heavy backpack.

By making the conscious choice to let go of pain, you are literally releasing stored negative energy. Some people experience a weight being lifted from them, others experience uncontrollable laughter.

Fear is temporary.

Mirror Work

Why is mirror work so important? Ask yourself these questions. How well do you know yourself? How do you relate to yourself? Do you meet yourself on an intimate level? Do you love yourself, forgive yourself, and reward yourself?

We have forgotten how to relate to ourselves on a deeper level. Mirror work brings us back to ourselves. It can be a difficult process meeting ourselves as you may have found out in the previous mirror work. I remember a time when I found it difficult to even see myself in the mirror, I hated myself so much. During my first session in front of the mirror I did the exercise looking down. Bit by bit though I was able to be with myself and start to value myself in a way I had never done before.

The following processes are designed to build new neural pathways so that we can relate to ourselves, respect ourselves and love ourselves. Once these neural pathways have been formed, our choices in life will be created with respect for ourselves, rather than chasing or trying to avoid something.

Repeat the mirror processes as often as you can, as the more you do them the quicker you will create the positive neural pathways.

Process – Relating to Yourself

Follow the instructions below.

1.   Sit in front of a mirror no more than a metre away so that you can see the whole of your face clearly.

2.   Look into your eyes.

3.   Say "I love and accept you."

4.   Open your heart to the person you see in the mirror.

5.   Say "It is OK, I am here for you and will not let you go."

6.   Say "I love and accept myself."

If you find it difficult to find the time or space in a busy household to do this, then do it every time you look in the mirror when in the bathroom. Just say "I love and accept you." If there are people around, just look at yourself and say it in your mind.

The next process further breaks down the barriers we have for ourselves by seeing ourselves as the giver and receiver of love. Some people are great at giving love and not great at receiving love. Others are great at receiving and not great at giving. This process creates the neural pathways for giving and receiving love.

Process – Receiving and Giving Love

Follow the instructions below.

1. Sit in front of a mirror no more than a metre away, so that you can see the whole of your face clearly.

2. Look at the person in front of you as if it were not you.

3. Say to them, "I love you."

4. Open your heart to the person you see in the mirror.

5. Say "It is OK, I am here for you and will not let you go."

6. Get up and walk away from the mirror for a second.

7. Go back to the mirror and sit down again.

8. This time you are the person in the mirror.

9. Say "I love you," still being the person in the mirror, receive the love. Really absorb the love given to you.

10. Say "It is OK, I am here for you and I will not let you down."

11. Still being the person in the mirror smile back at yourself knowing you are loved.

The Negative Voice

We all have a part of us that is bent on putting ourselves down. It is judgemental and tells us we are not good enough. It even judges others to make ourselves feel better.

Take a moment and listen to your negative voice. What is it saying about you right now? Maybe it is denying its existence. Become aware of what it is saying to you in the different situations in your life. We have become accustomed to listen to this negative voice. We take it very seriously, but it is not the truth. It is created out of fear of things we experienced in the past.

When our negative voice comes up wouldn't it be great to lessen its impact on us. Well there is a way that we can soften this voice and take it less seriously. The next time you hear your negative voice, repeat what it said, but imagine it has a funny squeaky voice. So if your voice said, "They wouldn't want to get to know me." Repeat the same words, but with the most ridiculous voice you can invent. It could be a cartoon character or maybe the voice of a favourite comedian. It must be funny though. This will create neural pathways that will enable you to take the voice in your head a little less seriously.

Another trick you can do with the voice is to imagine that it is coming from outside your head. Some people imagine it is sitting on their shoulder. You can then create the positive voice that is situated in your head. This voice can override what the negative voice is saying simply by being within your head. This one takes a bit of practice, so go easy on yourself if you can't do it straight away.

Our egos are great at judging other people. This causes the ego to feel that it is better than those people and thus makes us feel happier. This is a negative process and if we are unable to reduce this, then we are less likely to relate to people from a place of love and understanding. We are closed to them and this creates a way of being that keeps us from experiencing life to its fullest. The next time you feel that you are judging someone, simply remind yourself that this is just your lower self talking. You are operating from the ego. Try to imagine being the other person and how amazing it would feel if this authentic you accepted you fully.

Shame from School

For many of us, school was a traumatic experience and for others there were a few experiences that they'd rather forget about. Whatever it is for you, there will be something about school that left its imprint on you. In this process we will be recalling memories from school and hopefully finding some triggers and negative patterns. The way we do this is to actually act out something that happened at school. The next process may fit for you or it may not. The important thing is that you understand the process so that you can replicate it for a different situation.

Process – Recall School Memories

1. Find a corner of a room that has ample space to stand in.

2. Imagine you have been naughty at school and been told to stand in the corner.

3. Go and stand in the corner facing where the two walls meet. How does it feel? What does it invoke for you? Were you punished or humiliated at school?

This process is designed to bring any shame to the surface. We now know that the methods of punishment from yesteryear created shame for the children being punished. This shame needs to be acknowledged and released.

If this situation does not fit then rewrite the process to fit a situation that did happen. A common one was when the teacher asked a question and you put your hand up to answer. You were chosen and you confidently gave the answer. The next thing you know the whole class is laughing at you for getting the answer wrong. This is a big deal for a kid and that shame will still be with you. At the time you would not have wanted to cry or express any emotion, so you pushed it down. During this process you can safely express whatever you feel is right. You can scream, shout, get angry or cry. It is up to you, but it is important to express what you felt and release it.

Bullying

There is a good chance that you have experienced bullying or have been a bully at some point in your life. It is important to remember that bullies are just running patterns that enable them to feel good about themselves because they feel pretty worthless. No bully ever said, "I feel happy, confident, free, and loving." That's because anyone feeling this way would not be a bully as bullying is a response to very low self-esteem.

If you were a bully then forgive yourself. If there are people in your past that you need to apologise to, then it is a very good idea to do that. This will help remove the guilty feelings you hold onto even at a subconscious level.

If you were bullied try to put yourself in the shoes of the bully. Think about how low they must have felt to direct all that anger at you. If you need to get angry at them then use the anger process followed by the forgiveness process you learnt earlier. It is important that you release the anger and forgive them.

Self-Limiting Beliefs

Do you feel that you hold yourself back? Do you wonder why you keep failing in certain areas of your life? Do you find yourself procrastinating? Do you start to create or do something and then give up before it's finished? Do you feel uncomfortable in certain situations?

If you answered yes to any of these questions, then you probably have a self-limiting belief. This is a belief created somewhere in the past that you cannot do something or that it is not possible. You have neural pathways that were created affirming that you are set for failure. These could have been created by a parent, at school, your peers, or just because you failed at a few things when you were a child.

There is a process we can use to loosen the impact of these beliefs. First of all we must identify the belief. Where are you held back? What belief is holding you back? Another way to look at it is who would you be if you were to complete the task that is alluding you? What is stopping you being that person? Maybe you feel that you are not good enough. Maybe you believe you will always fail. Whatever it is, you have neural pathways that keep you locked in that belief. What we have to do is build some new neural pathways that will keep you believing that you can succeed.   Some limiting beliefs go deeper than you first think. For instance if your belief is that you would always be alone, then you must ask yourself, why do you think you will always be alone? The answer might be because nobody would want to love you. Then ask why no one would want to love you. If the answer is because you do not deserve love, or you are not worthy, then you probably have your belief. It always comes down to a very negative feeling you have about yourself. How does this limiting belief make you feel?

Common Self Limiting Beliefs

 I am worthless

I am unlovable

I am stupid

Now that we have a self-limiting belief we can start by weakening it. The next time you are aware of this self-limiting belief I want you to put it in the past tense. So if the belief is that you are not good enough then say, "In the past I used to believe that I wasn't good enough." If the belief was that you fail at everything then say, "I used to believe that I would fail at everything."

Next we are going to create a new belief that is the opposite of the self-limiting belief. If the old belief was that you were not good enough, then the new belief would be something like, "I am an unstoppable force and can achieve anything." If the old belief was that you always failed, then the new belief would be, "I am successful and can achieve anything."

Important: How does the new belief make you feel? Really tap into the emotion and get a sense of how it feels to be the belief.

Whenever the old belief comes up, replace it with the new belief. Keep doing this for as long as it takes. Remember the adage "Fake it till you make it." Keep going, keep forming those neural pathways. Eventually they will become solid and the new belief will hold.

Write your new belief on a piece of paper and stick it to your wall, or somewhere you see it every time you get in and out of bed.

How Do You See The Image Of Yourself

This is a great little process for shifting your perception of yourself. First we are going to look at how you see yourself and then at how you would like to see yourself. However you see yourself is written in to your neural pathways and this, like a self-limiting belief can be reversed.

When I first did this process the person I saw myself to be was all hunched over with my hands in my pockets looking uncomfortable. The new image I created for myself was a guy with legs slightly apart, standing upright with hands on his hips, smiling with his head in the air and looking up and into the distance. I was unstoppable. Once I had created this image I knew exactly what was possible.

Process – Self Image Change

1. Imagine what you look like to yourself when you are feeling disempowered. What image of yourself do you get? What does that image feel like?

2. Now create the image of the person you want to be. How are you situated? Are you lying, sitting, or standing? Are you smiling? Where are your hands? Do you look confident? If not then alter yourself so that you do.

3. How does it feel to be this person? Choose a power word that you associate with this new image of you. You will use this word in the next process.

4.   Each day remind yourself of this image.

Circle of Excellence

Now that you have a good image of yourself and some new unstoppable beliefs, it is time to introduce you to the circle of excellence. Each day you will rise to the circle of excellence and start the day with this new vision of you. This will further imprint the neural pathways with the new unstoppable you.

Process – Circle of Excellence

Either draw a circle on the floor next to your bed or cut out a piece of paper in the shape of a circle.

Every time you get out of bed step into the circle of excellence. Say your power word and remind yourself of your new image, your new positive beliefs and who you are being in the world.

Completing the Past

What ever happened in the past there is a very good chance that you upset someone along the way. There is also a good chance that someone upset you. There are neural pathways that you formed to deal with either of these scenarios. These pathways will have negative strands that may be affecting you and stopping you performing at your best. One of the most profound processes I have come across when dealing with stuff that happened in the past is revisiting it with the person involved and completing it.

You made a list earlier in the "Past Process." Choose one person off the list to start with.

It is important that when you proceed with this process you are blame free and are coming from a place of love and understanding. You now know that their and your actions were a result of years of negative programming. If you go into any conversation with even a tiny hint of blame then it will not end the way it is intended to for this process to work.

If you still have blame then there is more anger and forgiveness work to do. It is OK to have questions, but it is important that you word them in order that you are not blaming them.

For instance, my mother was never there for me as a child. The first time I attempted to talk to her about my childhood I asked her why she was not there for me. She got angry and told me she was there and that was the end of that conversation. After a bit of training I understood where I went wrong. The next time I had the conversation it went something like this.

"Can I talk to you about something mum?"

"Yes, what is it?"

"When I was a kid I felt like I was very alone. I am not blaming you for anything, as I know you must have had your own issues, but I just wanted to understand better what was going on."

She replied, "When your father left us he left us with nothing. I struggled to make ends meet. I was also depressed and was on antidepressants. I was tired a lot of the time. I found life very difficult."

In that moment I got it. I really saw how much my mother was struggling. So I went further.

"What was it like when you were growing up?" I asked.

"It was difficult being one of three sisters with two strict parents. They weren't very close to us and my father often used to slap the back of my head."

Again, it was all starting to fall in to place. My mother wasn't the evil witch I thought she was for all those years. She was just a product of her past and environment. I went into the conversation with full understanding and wanted to hear how life was for her. As you saw when I blamed her the first time the conversation was closed down.

Take some time to think about what you want to know. Word your sentences carefully. Avoid language that puts any onus on them. Come from a place of love and understanding. Then give them time to talk.

Be sure to get the timing right. You don't want to start the conversation while eating, or if they have just settled down to watch a film. If you are having the conversation over the phone, always check that they have time for a 20 minute conversation.

If you wronged the person tell them how sorry you are that you hurt them and explain to them why you did it. Remember to be honest. If it was because you were feeling insecure back then and you found it difficult to be a different way then you should tell them that rather than skimming over it. It is important that they really understand that you are sorry and that you are not that person anymore.

Process – Complete the Past

Choose one person from the list of people that have hurt you or that you have hurt.

Have a completion conversation as detailed above.

The Power of Giving

I found this out by chance when walking around London one day. The difference that it can make to your self-esteem is inspiring. I decided I was going to be generous and gave a homeless man £20. After I walked away I felt elated and happy. I then went to a large department store and just stood there holding the door open for a stream of people. I then went to get on a train. There were people pushing to get on. I stepped backwards and let them get on, whilst I got the next less crowded train. I felt good about myself. I was giving more than receiving. That evening I phoned a friend that I knew was having some difficulties in their life. I listened to them and did not add any of my own drama to it. They talked about their situation and how they were feeling and about all the possible outcomes. I offered a bit of advice when they asked for it. At the end of the conversation they said they felt understood and listened to. I felt good about myself. I had nothing to gain. I was just giving. And I felt great.

Process – Random Acts of Kindness

Find 3 random acts of kindness you can perform each week.

Re-framing Traumatic Events

When we are new to the world each new experience can be fraught with difficulties, clumsiness, or even trauma. We don't know how best to react to the emotions that arise in situations that we are not adept at dealing with. If we are unable to fully express our emotions then we swallow them down which can have a massive impact on the type of people we grow up to be. It can cause us anxiety and stress in future situations.

As I mentioned earlier, I worked on 13 incidents that involved my mother. It is hard to put into words how I felt afterwards, as I had carried this weight around with me my whole life. This weight was a feeling of not being quite at ease, a certain lack of confidence, a feeling that something would go wrong or I'd make a fool of myself. After I did the work re-framing these childhood events it was as if someone had taken a thick fog away from in front of me. I felt more at ease in situations that I used to find difficult. I was able to relax and talk more easily to people. I used to find it difficult to start a sentence and if I did say something I immediately shrank back into my shell, as I believed that people thought I was stupid or that they did not like me. Those years of negative bashing by my parents had formed the neural pathways that caused a fogginess and uncertainty about my interactions with people. I was literally petrified of making a fool of myself.

I worked through each of the events one at a time and my transformation was immediate. The confidence I felt was like nothing I had felt before and I was ready to test it out. I started talking to strangers, I made new friends, I was coming out of my shell.

Using the Re-framing process we are able to realign the memory of any traumatic or difficult event from the past so that its impact on us is significantly reduced. The more events you can find the better. Imagine all the events you experienced as a child. Each one is stacked upon a previous event. Each new experience is tainted by a previous experience. This stack of negativity can be completely removed, if you can find all the traumatic or upsetting situations you found yourself in as a child. Even if you only find a few events, working on these will significantly weaken their negative impact once you have reframed them.

Disassociating From the Event

When we experience anything in life we view it through our own senses. When we recall the memory it is almost always viewed through our own eyes as if we were the viewer. This is how it was written into our memory. We can vastly reduce the impact of recalling an event from the past, no matter how traumatic the event was, by simply changing our perspective.

For example, imagine you are sitting on a roller coaster. You have just sat down and the padded bar has just come down to keep you in your seat so that you do not fall out. The cars start moving and make their way up the steep slope towards the first drop. You can feel yourself being pushed into the back of your seat as gravity takes effect. You hear the click-click noise as the cars ascend. You feel the breeze on your face and get a sense of being high off the ground as you look around. You get to the top of the slope and the car returns to a horizontal position as you near the drop. There is a moment of silence as everyone anticipates the drop. Suddenly you are weightless, as the cars hurtle over the edge and you are now falling at a vast rate flying down the track.

As you experienced this event you were looking through your own eyes. Your senses were coming into play as your memory of the event was recalled. As you went over the edge you would have had a feeling of falling and maybe even some fear or excitement. Your memory of the event evoked feelings that were associated with the event. Using re-framing we are able to disassociate from the experience and reduce the negative impact that certain events have on us.

If you have never been on a roller coaster then imagine getting into a cold sea, river, or swimming pool. With each step you take you feel the cold pulsing through your body as you tense up slightly. Like the roller coaster, you are reliving the experience and evoking the feelings that were associated with the event, the uncomfortable moment as you shudder from the cold.

The first step in this process is to disassociate from the experience. This will disassociate us from the feelings that were present during the event.

Imagine you are sitting in a cinema. On the screen you can see yourself getting into a roller coaster car, or into some very cold water depending on which event you chose. Play out the same event from start to finish, but this time it is not through your own eyes, you are watching yourself play out the event on the movie screen. You will notice that the feelings previously associated with the event do not arise. We have disassociated from the experience and from the feelings. It is from this new perspective that we are going to change the movie and transform the negative feelings we once associated with the event. The neural pathways that once held a traumatic or upsetting state will be rewired to a happy and laughable state.

Rewriting the Memory

It is worth mentioning at this stage that some people prefer to reframe their experience in other ways than a movie. Some people like to paint an imaginary picture of the event, especially if they are a painter. Other techniques include, making clay models of the event, imagining driving down a street and seeing the events on billboards, or watching the event being acted out on stage in a theatre. Use whatever feels best for you. In my own experience I have found the movie to be most effective as it includes a timeline that you don't get with still pictures. For instance, I had a client that had a car crash in a remote location, followed by a traumatic ambulance ride. The event was played out over several hours. The movie was the best fit for her as it was important to transition from one situation to the other. Having said that, she could also have created still images of each of the traumatic incidents.

In order to change the memory we have to change some of the key ingredients of the memory when it was stored. We all store memories differently, whether it's more visual, auditory or something completely different. By simply changing the way we stored it can have a massive impact on how the memory affects us.

Below is a list of the things we can change within our memories :

Visual:
Black and White or colour / Near or Far / Bright or Dim / Location / Size of Picture / Focused or Unfocused / Moving or Still / Contrast / Flat or 3D

Auditory:
Location / Direction / Internal or External / Loud or Soft / Fast or Slow / High or Low Pitch / Tonality / Duration / Uniqueness of Sound / Clear or Muffled / Continuous or Discontinuous / Rhythm

Kinaesthetic (feeling):
Location / Size / Texture / Intensity / Movement / Temperature / Dry or Wet / Pressure / Weight

I once had a client that couldn't bare to recall the memory but could remember a colour, so we changed the colour to one she liked and before we knew we had rewritten the memory.

We can also change the actual events within the movie. For instance, I had a client that was attacked so we changed the actions between her and her attacker in to a dance. We can also put smiles on the faces of the people within the movie. We can make people clowns, or imagine them wearing silly clothes. We could even turn them into animals. The way you change the movie is up to you in the moment. If you were crying then see yourself laughing. No matter how terrible the movie looks we can change it to something positive.

Process – Re-framing Traumatic events

First of all, we need to think of a traumatic event. You may only have one, you may have many. Write a list of as many traumatic events that you can remember from your past. They may be as far back as when you were born or even just a few days ago, this process works no matter how old the memory is.

Next rate each memory from one to ten, ten being the most traumatic and write that number next to the memory on the list.

Choose a memory with a rating over 7 or the highest on your list.

Find somewhere comfortable to sit and read these instructions before you start so that you can work with the memory without re-reading the instructions but don't worry if you do need a recap.

Imagine you are sitting on a chair in front of a big screen. Now imagine you are floating out of your body and you are now watching yourself in the chair watching the screen.

On the screen you can see the memory start to be played out. You can see yourself on the screen. Play the movie from start to finish, the finish being the last thing you remember from the event.

Now that you have a good idea of what the movie looks like make a mental note of the visual, auditory, and kinaesthetic elements of the movie.

Play the movie again and try changing one or two of these elements. For instance, if it was raining you could make it a sunny day, if it was very quiet you could imagine a brass band playing, if someone was looking ominous then you could make them look like a person in a fancy dress costume, perhaps or cartoon character. You could even imagine it was all being played out on stage by some actors in a comedy play.

You are in complete control of how you re-write your memories. The more effort you put in to each one the less of a negative impact it will have on you. Just remember that it's all happening on the screen in front of you not as if you were seeing it through your own eyes.

When you are happy with the new version of events then think about how you now rate that memory from one to ten and write the number next to the old number. If you think you could get the number lower then try a new rewrite. Most people get down to a rating of two after just a couple of rewrites.

The Beginning

Well done, you made it to the end of this book and you hopefully used all the processes listed here. By now you are feeling a new lease of life and wish to be out in the world with this new confidence. The first thing you could do is buy a copy of this book and give it to a friend that you think could really benefit from it. The more people within your network that are operating from their happiest self the happier life will be for all those around them.

This is the beginning of a new, happier, healthier, awesome version of you. Remember to do your affirmations every week and use the processes within this book every few months if you feel you need a top up.

The 12 Karmic Laws

I am including the 12 Karmic Laws in this workbook as a guide and reference. These precepts have been used for thousands of years in the Far East. They have helped me to stay focussed and reminded me of what I need to change to remain a happy and stable person.

THE GREAT LAW
As you sow, so shall you reap. This is also known as the Law of Cause and Effect. Whatever we put out in the Universe is what comes back to us.

If what we want is Peace, Friendship, Happiness, Love...

Then we should BE Peaceful, Loving, Happy, a Friend.

THE LAW OF CREATION
Life doesn't just happen, it requires our participation. We are one with the Universe. Whatever surrounds us gives us our inner state.

BE what you want to have in your Life.

THE LAW OF HUMILITY
What you resist will persist.

If what we see is that which we find to be negative, then we are not focused on a higher level of existence.

THE LAW OF GROWTH

Wherever you go, there you are. For us to grow in Spirit it is we who must change and not the people, places or things around us. The only given we have in our lives is ourselves and that is the only factor we have control over.

When we change who and what we are within our heart our life changes too.

THE LAW OF RESPONSIBILITY

Whenever there is something wrong, there is something wrong in me.

We must take responsibility for what is in our life.

THE LAW OF CONNECTION

Even if something we do seems inconsequential, it is very important that you do it, as everything in the Universe is connected. Each step leads to the next step.

Neither the first step nor the last are of greater significance

THE LAW OF FOCUS

You can't think of two things at the same time.

When our focus is on Spiritual Values, it is impossible for us to have lower thoughts that lead to selfishness.

THE LAW OF GIVING AND HOSPITALITY

If you believe something to be true, then sometime in your life you will be called upon to demonstrate that truth.

Here is where we put what we SAY that we have learned into PRACTICE.

THE LAW OF HERE AND NOW

Looking back to examine what was, prevents us from being totally in the HERE AND NOW. Old thoughts, old patterns of behaviour, leave us living in the past and prevent us from having new ones.

THE LAW OF CHANGE

History repeats itself until we learn the lessons that we need to change our path.

THE LAW OF PATIENCE AND REWARD

All Rewards require initial toil. Rewards of lasting value require patient and persistent toil.

True Joy follows doing what we're supposed to be doing and waiting for the Reward to come in it's on time.

THE LAW OF SIGNIFICANCE AND INSPIRATION

You get back from something, whatever you've put into it. The Value of something is a direct result of the energy and intent that is put into it.

Every personal contribution is also a contribution to the Whole.